BEATING
THE BENZO BLUES
GETTING OFF BENZODIAZEPINES

DALE CARRUTH

Beating the Benzo Blues

Getting off Benzodiazepines.

by Dale Carruth

Copyright © 2021 Dale Carruth. All rights reserved. 2021. No part of this book may be reproduced by any means, including photocopying, or stored or transmitted by any means without advance clearance from Dale Carruth, Queensland Australia. 1st Edition.

Editing by T. von Oberstockstall

Published by Dale Carruth - 3feathersbooks@gmail.com

Cover Art by Dale Carruth

ISBN:978-0-6453249-0-7 print

ISBN:978-0-6453249-1-4 epub

ISBN:978-0-6453249-2-1 mobi

Dewey Number:

Subjects: Benzodiazepines - Prescription Medication Addiction – Sleeping Pills – Anxiolytics – Prescription Medication Detoxification – Addiction - Valium – Drug Withdrawal Symptoms – Drugs - Anxiety – Insomnia – Tranquilisers.

1st Edition

Printed by Ingram Spark

CONTENTS

1. Introduction 6
2. What are Benzodiazepines? 9
3. The Problems with Benzodiazepines 14
4. Benzodiazepine withdrawal symptoms. 19
5. Common withdrawal symptoms explained 22
6. Commonly asked questions 24
7. Self-care for people withdrawing from benzodiazepines 27
8. Detoxing off Benzo's - A Three Step Process 36
9. Support 49
10. Advice to Health Professionals 51
11. Judy's Story 55
12. Marcus's Story 57
13. Useful Books & Journal Articles 59

BEATING THE BENZO BLUES

Getting off Benzodiazepines

by Dale Carruth

Acknowledgements: I would like to acknowledge that some of the content used in this booklet has come from:

Shirley Trickett: *Coming off tranquillisers, sleeping pills and anti-depressants*, (1998) Thorson's Publishers, Great Britain.

Larry Neild: *Escape from Tranquillisers and Sleeping Pills.* (1990) Random House, Great Britain.

Tranx Services Auckland; Clinical Staff and Manager; Shaz Picard.

INTRODUCTION

This book is intended for people who are considering stopping the use of benzodiazepines or have been advised to do so by their doctor. It provides information on these drugs and the problems that can arise when stopping their use. It gives specific information on managing withdrawal and living life in the process. It is important to realise that reducing from benzodiazepines is a process not an event.

The words, 'benzodiazepines' 'benzos' and 'minor tranquillisers' refer to the same drugs. The words 'addiction' and 'dependence,' for the purpose of this book have the same meaning. This book is specifically for people who have been taking benzodiazepines to manage anxiety or sleeping problems. Benzodiazepines are also prescribed for other medical conditions such as certain forms of epilepsy and disorders that cause muscle spasm. I am not suggesting that people who use benzodiazepines for these purposes stop the use of their drugs. However, in this instance it may help with reduction (lower dose) and management.

To summarise, this booklet is for you if you:

- think you might be addicted to benzodiazepines
- know you are addicted to benzodiazepines
- are currently reducing from benzodiazepines
- have a doctor that has advised you to come off benzodiazepines
- are using benzodiazepines for anxiety or sleep disorders

WHAT ARE BENZODIAZEPINES?

History

Benzodiazepines were introduced in the early 1960s and were thought to be a safer alternative to the barbiturate drugs commonly prescribed at the time for sleep and anxiety disorders. Benzodiazepines were intensively marketed by Purdue pharmaceuticals as a remedy for psychic tension and said to be virtually free from side effects and potential for addiction. We now know that this was not true - they are highly addictive drugs, and the side effects are numerous. Benzodiazepines are responsible for one of the worst medical blunders of the twentieth century, with millions of people world-wide suffering emotional and physical illness, because they took these drugs in prescribed therapeutic doses.

The Sackler brothers, the owners of Purdue, started their empire in 1952 with the purchase of Purdue Pharmaceuticals. They co-authored over 100 papers on the biochemistry of mental illness. By using these papers, they were able to convince the Journal of American Medical Association to run a full colour add to market Valium. Purdue was the first company to achieve over 100 million in sales for a single drug (Valium) which got Arthur Sackler inducted into the medical advertising hall of fame.

Valium is a highly addictive benzodiazepine, and now a controlled drug in many countries due to its high addiction potential. The Sackler's falsely marketed it as a drug for all kinds of ailments under the umbrella term of psychic tension, when it should have only have been prescribed for anxiety and chronic insomnia.

When patients reported feeling anxious and unwell after stopping the use of these supposedly non-addictive drugs, it was thought their original anxiety problem had returned. It was not recognised then that these symptoms were drug withdrawal symptoms. Patients were told to go back on their drugs, and the symptoms eased. Therefore, people continued to take them year after year. Some people have taken benzodiazepines for twenty years or more. After many years of controversy, media coverage, and patients taking legal action over these drugs, the attitude of the medical profession has now considerably changed.

Controlled drug legislation - NZ

On the 1st January 1999, the New Zealand Ministry of Health issued notification to all health professionals that Benzodiazepines would now be classified as a Class C, Controlled Drug. Therefore, Benzodiazepines are now controlled under the Misuse of Drugs Act (1975). This was part of a world-wide initiative to reduce the number of benzodiazepines being diverted from legal to elicit channels. Benzodiazepine consumption are now subject to controls on prescription, particularly prescription for the treatment of chemical dependence.

NZ Doctors were made answerable and had to become

gazetted with the Ministry of Health when prescribing benzodiazepines for the treatment of addiction. If a doctor was aware that a person was seeking benzodiazepines because of addiction (i.e., seeking increasing doses) then that patient must be referred to a gazetted clinic, and put on a reduction regime.

Types of Benzodiazepines

Benzodiazepines are minor tranquillisers; a group of drugs, usually prescribed to relieve anxiety or to promote sleep. There are essentially two types of benzodiazepines - **anxiolytics** prescribed for anxiety and **sedative-hypnotics** prescribed for sleeplessness and insomnia. There are about 54 different drugs, which make up the family of benzodiazepines. The table below shows the commonly prescribed in New Zealand. Benzodiazepines have both a generic name and a trade name.

How they Work

Benzodiazepines work by increasing the effects of a neurotransmitter (chemical messenger) in the brain called *gamma*-aminobutyric acid (GABA). The actions of GABA are of an inhibitory nature, i.e., they reduce brain activity. This leads to reduced muscle tension, less anxiety and a general slowing down or sedation. Benzodiazepines differ in the speed with which they start to work and the length of time they continue to have an effect. Some take effect within minutes, whereas others take several hours to have a noticeable effect. They also differ in the duration of their effect. Some last for only a few hours while others remain effective for many hours.

Benzodiazepines Commonly Prescribed in NZ.

Generic (Chemical) Name	Brand Name
Alprazolam	Xanax
Lorazepam	Lorzem, Ativan, Lorapam
Oxazepam	Ox-Pam, Serapax, Benzotram
Chlordiazepoxide	Nova-Pam, (Librium)
Clobazam	Frisium
Lormetazepam	Noctamid
Triazolam	Halcion, Trycam
Temazepam	Euhypnos, Normison, Somapam
Nitrazepam	Insoma, Nitrados, (Mogadon)
Diazepam	D-Pam, Pro-Pam, (Valium)
Clonazepam	Rivotril

Note: Brand Names in brackets are no longer produced under these names.

Zopiclone (Imovane) *is a commonly prescribed minor tranquilliser. It's not considered a benzodiazepine therefore it's not a controlled drug. However, it causes the same problems as benzodiazepine **sedative-hypnotics**, and is definitely addictive.*

In Britain prescriptions for Imovane rose from 2000 in 1993 to 2.25 million in 1999.

It was listed as schedule IV in the USA in 2005 due to evidence that it has addictive properties similar to benzodiazepines.

*In NZ, by 2020 it is the most widely dispensed, funded **sedative-hypnotics**. The number of people dispensed Zopiclone (Imovane) in the 12 months from October 2019 to Sept 2020 was greater than the total number of people dispensed any benzodiazepine. This is obviously a result of the fact that it's not classed as a benzodiazepine, so it bypasses the controlled drug category requirements.*

THE PROBLEMS WITH BENZODIAZEPINES

Taken correctly, benzodiazepines can be very helpful drugs. They can relieve the symptoms of acute anxiety and give the sufferer a much-needed reprieve. They can offer relief during a difficult short-term crisis such as bereavement.

Benzodiazepines are effective and relatively safe drugs when used for short periods of time, intermittently, and in low doses. The therapeutic time frame for benzodiazepines is approximately eight weeks.

Problems with Benzodiazepines

- they lose their effectiveness
- they are addictive
- they have withdrawal effects
- they have side effects
- they cause feelings of a drugged state
- they don't mix well with other medications
- use during pregnancy may harm your baby
- elderly people are more sensitive to the effects

They lose their effectiveness

Tolerance occurs when the prescribed dose no longer achieves the desired effect. A larger dose may then be required to achieve the same effect. Increased tolerance to some benzodiazepines may take as little as three days. *You can experience withdrawal symptoms while still taking your prescribed pills.* Many people who have taken benzodiazepines have become tolerant, and because they have not increased their dose over the months or years, they may experience withdrawal symptoms, despite taking their prescribed dose.

They are addictive

Benzodiazepines are addictive. Addiction occurs when a person feels like they can't live without the drug. This can happen in as little as four to six weeks. When you take a substance such as alcohol, benzodiazepines, or caffeine, your body must adjust to cope with it. If it then relies on the introduced substance to function normally, the result is chemical dependence or addiction.

They have withdrawal effects

If you have become addicted to benzodiazepines, or you stop using them suddenly, you may experience serious withdrawal symptoms. <u>If you have been using benzodiazepines for more than a few weeks, do not suddenly cease using them without contacting a knowledgeable counsellor, or seeking medical advice.</u> Benzodiazepines should be gradually reduced over a period of time, in consultation with a counsellor or a doctor.

They have side effects

Like many other drugs, benzodiazepines may cause side effects in some people. The most common ones noted are drowsiness, lethargy, dry mouth, light-headedness, headache, irritability, nausea, upset stomach, constipation, or diarrhoea. These symptoms may be side effects of benzodiazepine use, or they may be caused by something else. Also, after a period of time benzodiazepines may cause the very symptoms, they were prescribed for: anxiety, panic and insomnia.

They cause feelings of a drugged state

Benzodiazepines may cause the user to feel sedated, foggy, and somewhat removed from reality. Emotional desensitisation may also occur. Friends and relatives may notice personality changes in the user due to their benzodiazepine use.

They don't mix well with alcohol or other medications

Benzodiazepines should not be mixed with alcohol or other medications as this can cause harmful reactions. Alcohol, like benzodiazepines, is a central nervous system (CNS) depressant and can increase the sedating effect of the drug. Driving is especially dangerous when the two drugs are taken together.

Use during pregnancy may harm your baby.

Taking benzodiazepines during pregnancy appears to increase the risk of birth defects and respiratory illnesses in the baby. They can also pass through the breast milk, causing drowsiness and possible withdrawal symptoms in the baby.

Elderly people are more sensitive to the effects of benzodiazepines

The effects of these drugs last longer in the elderly. Loss of balance, falls and confusion are more common because of taking benzodiazepines. It was estimated in 2020 that 10% of all people over age 70 are taking prescribed benzodiazepines in NZ.

Important Points To Remember

1. Don't stop taking benzodiazepines without seeking medical advice or contacting a specialist counsellor. To do so could be dangerous.

2. Continuous use of benzodiazepines is more likely to lead to addiction than intermittent use.

3. Four to six months is the danger period for addiction to benzodiazepines. However, some people have become addicted in four weeks or less.

4. Sleeping pills are as likely to cause addiction as anti-anxiety agents.

5. Addiction can and does occur when taking low or therapeutic doses of benzodiazepines.

6. Withdrawal symptoms can occur while people are taking prescribed amounts of benzodiazepines.

7. Alcohol should not be taken with benzodiazepines or during withdrawal. They are both CNS depressants and have an additive effect.

BENZODIAZEPINE WITHDRAWAL SYMPTOMS.

It is important to know that any withdrawal symptoms you have are not permanent. They will go away when your body becomes accustomed to withdrawal from the drug. The following list will help you recognise what you may experience if you are in withdrawal. Most people will experience only some of these symptoms. If you experience a lot of these symptoms, it could be an indication that you are reducing too quickly, or not looking after your health. It's recommended that you get a full physical check-up to rule out other possibilities.

The following is a list of symptoms experienced and reported by people who have been addicted to benzodiazepines. Many people experience some of these symptoms while still on their prescribed dose of benzodiazepines. This usually indicates that their bodies have developed a tolerance to the pills. Symptoms may also occur within 21 - 24 hours after ceasing or reducing benzodiazepines, but they can occur as late as the second week after reduction or cessation. Benzodiazepines act on the brain and central nervous system, which control all the systems of the body. In withdrawal, all parts of the body are affected.

Common Benzodiazepine Withdrawal Symptoms.

Physical

Nausea	Abdominal pain
Constipation	Diarrhoea
Distorted or blurred vision	Dizziness
Sweating	Shaking
Palpitations	Slow pulse
Tight chest	Chest pain
Headaches	Sinus problems
Pain in the neck and shoulders	Rashes

Emotional

Aggression	Increased anxiety
Increased depression	Mood swings
Panic attacks	Hyperactivity
Agoraphobia	Confusion
Suicidal feelings	Fear of going mad
Outbursts of rage	

Sleep

Insomnia	Nightmares
Disturbed sleep	Night sweats

Senses

Metallic taste in mouth	Sensitivity to light/sound
Pins and needles	Numbness
Creeping, skin sensations	Ringing in ears
Loss of taste	Hallucinations (seeing or hearing things)

Common Benzodiazepine Withdrawal Symptoms.

Senses

Tight band around head	Feelings of electricity all over

Other

Fatigue or lack of energy	Loss of appetite
Impotence	Lack of interest in sex
Increase in sexual feelings	Hormonal problems
Thyroid problems	Fits
Jelly legs	Alopecia (hair loss)
Breathlessness	

COMMON WITHDRAWAL SYMPTOMS EXPLAINED

Depression: Most drug withdrawal is associated with depression. You may feel useless, empty, hopeless, sad, and tearful. You may have little interest in life or things that used to give you enjoyment. This may be caused by a chemical reaction in your brain or because you must face feelings that have been artificially suppressed by the drugs. It will pass. Try to focus on stopping negative thoughts. Writing gratitude lists can help. Give yourself time and be gentle with yourself. Follow the advice you would give to your own best friend if they were feeling like you.

Panic Attacks: Feelings of intense anxiety often associated with a sense of impending doom or disaster and a fear of going mad. This is often accompanied by uncomfortable physical symptoms, which include: palpitations, nausea, dizziness, shaking, feelings of unreality, pins and needles, and hot and cold flushes. These attacks can last seconds, minutes or hours. They are unpleasant but not dangerous. Try doing the breathing exercises suggested below.

Suicidal Feelings: Can occur when anxiety levels are high. These usually disappear when anxiety levels drop, but it is essential to see your doctor or let your counsellor know if you are having such feelings. There are mental health crisis teams available in every area. To contact these teams call your local hospital.

Insomnia: This is the inability to sleep. It can be severe in withdrawal and may continue for months. It will get better in time. You can help yourself in a few of the following ways. Don't drink coffee or other caffeinated drinks close to bedtime. Drink herbal teas instead. (Camomile is good). Do relaxation exercises, breathing exercises, or meditation. Taking benzodiazepines deprives the user of dream (REM) sleep. In withdrawal you may be flooded with vivid dreams or nightmares. These can often be of a disturbing nature. Although difficult, try to accept that this is a good sign. Your brain is starting to work again. Remember that one hour of deep relaxation is better for you than hours of restless sleep.

COMMONLY ASKED QUESTIONS

Do all users become addicted?

The answer to this is no. The reason why some people become addicted, and some do not is not clearly understood. It is possible that the people who do become addicted to benzodiazepines are allergic to them.

Have I damaged myself permanently through taking benzodiazepines?

Many people ask this question. It is important to know that the human body has an amazing capacity for punishment and recovery. Once the drug leaves your body, things will slowly return to normal. There is a wealth of support and information available, so you don't have to do it alone.

How do I know if I am addicted?

If you feel sick, shaky, high, anxious, or depressed when you try to cut down your pills, and if the feelings go away when you take them again, you could be addicted. If you find you are needing increasing doses you have probably developed a tolerance which is another clear sign of addiction.

What do I do if I think I might be addicted?

There are several options: You can organise an appointment with a knowledgeable addiction counsellor or clinic who can work alongside you while reducing. You could contact your doctor or health professional and discuss your concerns. Remember that some doctors are well informed on benzodiazepine withdrawal and will support you all the way. Others know very little about benzodiazepine withdrawal and will encourage you to seek other specialist help. Still others may suggest you just stay on them because you need them or will suggest you just stop taking them. **If the latter happens, I strongly suggest you get another opinion.**

How long will the withdrawal symptoms last?

There is no easy answer to this question because it greatly varies. It will depend on the particular drug you have been on, how long you have taken it, and how long it takes your body to get back to normal. This can depend on your age and other medical conditions.

What causes withdrawal symptoms?

Benzodiazepines make you less anxious, you sleep better, your heart rate and breathing are slower, your movements and thinking are slower, your emotions are pushed down, you feel less, your senses are dulled, your muscles relaxed, blood sugar levels are high: *essentially your adrenaline levels are low.* When you reduce benzodiazepines too quickly, your anxiety soars, you can't sleep, your heart rate and breathing speed up, your thoughts race, you become hyperactive, your trapped emotions come pouring out, your muscles tighten and hurt, your blood sugar falls: *your adrenaline levels are high.* Clinical tests show that after the drugs have been stopped, adrenaline levels can rise to six times higher than the pre-withdrawal levels. Is it not surprising that people feel like they are going mad?

I am taking both benzodiazepines and anti-depressants: should I come off both at the same time?

It is recommended that you withdraw from your benzodiazepines first, then wait until you feel settled before withdrawing from your anti-depressants.

SELF-CARE FOR PEOPLE WITHDRAWING FROM BENZODIAZEPINES

Be patient and nurturing with yourself. Help your body by exercising and eating healthy food. Take time out and do relaxation and breathing exercises. Try to stay positive and don't spend time dwelling on negative thoughts. Live in the day. If you have spiritual beliefs, now is the time to enlist the help of your Higher Power or God, and practise prayer and meditation. Keep a journal and write down your thoughts and feelings. Try to maintain some routine in your life. Before you go to bed at night, write a small list of things to do tomorrow. This will give you some focus for the day, as people in withdrawal often feel disorganised and confused. Tick things off as you achieve them. This will give you a satisfied feeling of having achieved something for the day. Be realistic and don't aim too high.

Alternative Therapies

Many people have been helped both during and after withdrawal by various alternative therapies, including: massage, herbal medicine, homeopathy, acupuncture, micro-dosing psilocybin mushrooms or other psychedelics.

Massage

Great for relieving stress and muscular aches and pains, which are often present during withdrawal. It is also a nurturing time out, to be pampered and relax.

Herbal Medicine

A restorative tonic can be made up especially for you to cater to your specific needs and symptoms. Find a qualified Herbalist, Chinese Medicine Practitioner, or a Pharmacist who specialises in drug detoxification.

Reading

Learn about withdrawal. I have included a list of useful books at the end of this booklet. I recommend that you find out as much as possible about what you are going through. If you have full information about your symptoms, you are likely to feel more reassured that what you are going through is normal. It is empowering to take responsibility for your own recovery and do as much as you can to help yourself.

Friends and Family

Explain to your friends and family what you are going through and what you are doing about it. Show them any information that you have. They are likely to be more supportive than you think and will feel better if they know what is happening. The more support you have the better. Partners can often gain a lot by being involved in your process.

Relaxation Exercises

Relaxation exercises should be done in the morning and before your evening meal. Remember that you are not just lying there being lazy; rather you are allowing your breathing to slow, your heart to rest, your muscles to relax and increasing stimulation to the brain. You are giving your body the best possible natural tranquilliser. Find a good relaxation recording, avoid ones which use the "tighten and let go" method of muscle relaxation. This can cause muscle cramps in people who are withdrawing.

Breathing Exercises

Try to do these exercises twice a day; after breakfast and before you're evening meal. Sessions should take at least half an hour. These exercises are especially good if you are having panic attacks or agoraphobia. A quick five minutes here and there is not enough. Try to stick to the recommended time of 30 minutes. Sit comfortably in a chair or lie on the floor or a bed. Loosen any tight clothing. When you become more skilled you should be able to do these exercises anywhere, even standing in a queue. The aim is to breathe slowly lifting the abdomen. If you breathe too deeply, you can become lightheaded.

Practise this until you feel you can do it readily:

1. Place one hand on your stomach and one on your chest. The hand on your chest should stay as still as possible. The hand on your stomach will rise and fall as you breathe.

2. Breathe out through your nose gently and let your stomach fall as you do.

3. Breathe in through the nose, letting your stomach rise. Make the out breath longer than the in breath.

4. You should aim at doing these eight to twelve times per minute.

Exercise

You don't have to get carried away and prepare for the next marathon. Light and regular is the key. Walking is great; it gets you out in the fresh air and sunshine. Stretch-Yoga is a fantastic stress reliever and releases muscle tension in your body. It stimulates the circulation, which will help flush the drugs out of your system. There are many Yoga studios around. There are also a variety of YouTube videos on yoga, if you prefer to practise in the sanctuary of your own home and at your own pace.

Vitamin and Mineral Supplements

Many people who have taken benzodiazepines over long time periods usually have severe vitamin and mineral deficiencies. It is known that benzodiazepines block zinc absorption. They probably hinder the absorption of other vital nutrients too. A healthy diet will help. Natural vitamins from fresh and raw food are a good starting point. However, getting the correct supplements can speed your recovery. Some common signs to watch out for that usually signify vitamin deficiencies: Bleeding gums, mouth ulcers, recurrent herpes, gum boils, swollen or sore tongue, spontaneous bruising, slow healing cuts, falling and lifeless hair, cramps, yeast infections or thrush. There are some good books available on nutritional medicine or you could seek your doctor's advice. I recommend a good multi-vitamin, a B complex supplement, Zinc and Vitamin D.

Diet

Many drugs, including benzodiazepines, raise blood sugar levels. When the level of the drug in the blood stream drops, the blood sugar also falls. There is often confusion between drug withdrawal symptoms and hypoglycaemia (low blood sugar) symptoms. Hypoglycaemia and withdrawal symptoms both include headaches, anxiety, depression, shaking etc. While it is difficult to separate these symptoms, it is clear that people who maintain a low blood sugar diet while withdrawing will dramatically reduce their withdrawal symptoms, and are more likely to complete their withdrawal and not feel the need to turn to other substances.

Principles of a Low Blood Sugar Diet: The aim of this diet is to avoid rapid changes in the level of glucose in the blood because this increases the level of adrenaline in the body.

Food and Drink to Avoid

Chocolate	Sugar	Junk foods
Sweets	White bread	Sweet drinks
Cakes	White flour	Alcohol
Biscuits	Pastry	

Best Food to Eat

Non-Refined Carbohydrates:

Whole Grain	Oats	Barley
Cereals	Pasta	Millet
Rice		

Protein:

Meat	Fish	Poultry
Eggs	Milk	Cheese
Yoghurt		

Vegetable Protein:

Nuts	Seeds	Beans
Lentils	Peas	

Eat plenty of fresh raw fruit:

Although fruit contains quite a lot of sugar, it is in a fructose form. It does not need insulin for its digestion; therefore, it is an ideal food to slow down the pancreas.

Eat lots of raw and cooked vegetables:

This will provide you with essential vitamins and minerals and provide roughage. Raw food is nutritionally better than cooked food. It is easier to digest and most importantly for people in withdrawal, the enzymes work to clean toxins out of the cells.

Drink plenty of water:

This helps to flush toxins out of your system. Eight glasses a day is the recommended minimum.

- Carrots have been called the most therapeutic food in the world. This root vegetable really is an amazing antidote for stress. Eat raw as a snack or drink as a juice.

- Lettuce is a natural tranquilliser? It contains a chemical called lactucin, which helps to induce a relaxed state.

- Raw cabbage is packed with vitamin C, one of the most important vitamins

- Cucumbers and string beans are rich in potassium, one of the most important minerals.

- Grapes help to detoxify the body and provide instant energy. Black grapes are best.

- Sunflower seeds are packed with nutrients such as iron, vitamin E and B. These seeds have a sedating effect. Keep a supply in your bag as an emergency snack. Add in a few pumpkin seeds for variety.

- Beetroot can alleviate menstrual problems. Grated, it adds taste and colour to a salad.

- Celery contains a multitude of minerals.

- Pecan nuts are one of the best-known sources of natural pyridoxine (vitamin B6)

- Bananas are packed with minerals - potassium and magnesium. They are rich in tryptophan, an amino acid, which promotes sleep.

- Mangoes are great anti-depressants.

- Turkey is packed with tryptophan. A turkey sandwich is a great snack.

- Rolled Oats are an underrated health food. They're one of the best tonics for the nervous system. They build stamina and energy and have been credited with helping depression.

- Wheatgerm oil is a good source of vitamin E.

DETOXING OFF BENZO'S - A THREE STEP PROCESS

1. Split Your Current Daily Dose
2. Change over to Diazepam
3. Reduce According to the Guide

Step 1: Split your current daily dose: Identify the effectiveness time frame of the particular drug you are on by using the following chart. Then you will need to split your daily dose up so that you're not going in and out of withdrawal throughout the day. You may need to get a pill cutter (available from most chemists) to cut your pills up.

Half-life vs Effectiveness

Be aware: There's a big difference between Half Life and Effectiveness. Half-life refers to how long the drug is traceable in your system through a blood test. Effectiveness refers to how long it actually works to relieve your symptoms.

Half-life VS Effectiveness

Approved Name	Brand Name	Half-life (hours)	Effectiveness (hours)
Triazolam (sedative-hypnotic)	Halcion	2	.5
Zopiclone (Non-Benzo sedative-hypnotic)	Imovane	5 - 6	2
Temazepam (sedative-hypnotic)	Normison	8 - 22	3.5
Oxazepam (anti-anxiety)	Serepax	4 - 15	1.5
Alprazolam (anti-anxiety)	Xanax	6 - 12	3
Lorazepam (anti-anxiety)	Ativan	10 - 12	4
Diazepam (anti-anxiety and sedative)	Valium	20 - 100	8
Clonazepam (anti-anxiety)	Rivotril	24 - 120	8

Example 1: Split doses Oxazapam (Serapax)

Aim: To reduce withdrawal symptoms
Occurs: During Assessment
Case Example: Client is on Oxazepam 60 mg daily; taken as 30 mg twice daily. (Anti-anxiety)
Daily Dose: 60 mg
Half-life: 4-15 hours
Effectiveness: 1.5 hours
Tablet sizes (mg): 10, 15, 30

Using 10 mg tablets

7am	9am	11am	1pm	3pm	5pm	7pm	9pm	11pm	
10 mg	5 mg	5 mg	5 mg	5 mg	5 mg	5 mg	10 mg	10 mg	= 60 mg

Using 15mg tablets

7am	9.30am	12pm	2.30pm	5pm	7.30pm	10pm	
7.5 mg	7.5 mg	7.5 mg	7.5 mg	7.5 mg	7.5 mg	15 mg	= 60 mg

Using 30mg (not commonly prescribed)

7am	12pm	5pm	10pm	
15 mg	15 mg	15 mg	15 mg	= 60 mg

Example 2: Split Doses Imovane (Zopiclone)

Aim: To reduce withdrawal symptoms

Occurs: During Assessment

Case Example: Client presents on Imovane (Non-benzodiazepine sedative-hypnotic) taken at night 22.5 mg.

Daily Dose: 22.5 mg

Half Life: 6.5 hours

Effectiveness: Two hours

Tablet Size: 7.5 mg

8 am	11 am	2 pm	5 pm	10 pm	
3.75 mg	3.75 mg	3.75 mg	3.75 mg	7.5 mg	= 22.5 mg

Imovane is a sleeping tablet so it's important to keep the night-time dose topped up.

Changeover to Diazepam

Diazepam is a **long-acting** benzodiazepine.

1. It has approximately eight hours of effectiveness. Four doses daily, every 4 – 6 hours, accumulates during the day and holds the client stable during the night so they don't wake up in withdrawal.

> Contrast Imovane: Effectiveness two hours.
>
> An addicted client would need to take a dose every two hours, (including during the night) to keep withdrawal symptoms from occurring.

2. Diazepam is both an anxiolytic and a sedative-hypnotic. (It has both an anti-anxiety and a sedative effect)

3. Diazepam comes in 10, 5, and 2 mg tablets. It is easier for clients to reduce by 1mg by cutting a 2mg tablet in half.

> Contrast Imovane: It comes in 7.5 mg tablets. It's extremely difficult for a client to reduce this tablet by 1 mg.

Changeover Procedure (Mono Drug User)

- Step 1: Stabilise on your current drug by splitting the doses throughout the day depending on its effectiveness. (Doses are split to alleviate withdrawal symptoms).

- Step 2: Changeover to Diazepam. This process varies depending on whether they are on a sedative-hypnotic or anxiolytic. This process usually takes around ten days.

- Stabilise for two weeks on Diazepam.

- Step 3: Reduction regime begins. This is a very individual process.

- Rate of reduction for long time users (seven years or more) is on average, a month for every year they have been consuming them.

- Stabilisation happens throughout the reduction process.

- It may be best to have a trusted therapist to monitor you throughout your reduction process to provide counselling. Emotions will generally present themselves as your reduction process progresses.

Dose Equivalents to Diazepam

Approved Name	Brand Name	Half-life	Dose Equiv. to 10 mg Diazepam
Alprazolam	Xanax	6–12	1 mg
Chlordiazepoxide	Nova Pam	5-30 (36-200)	25 mg
Clobazam	Frisium	12-60	20 mg
Diazepam	D Pam, Propam	20-100 (36- 200)	10 mg
Flunitrazepam	Rohypnol	20-30 (36-200)	1 mg
Lorazepam	Ativan	10-20	2 mg
Lormetazepam	Noctamid	10-12	2 mg
Nitrazepam	Insoma, Nitrados	15-38	10 mg
Oxazepam	Serapax, Benzotian	4-15	20 mg
Temazepam	Normison Euhypnos	8-22	20 mg
Triazolam	Halcion, Hypam	2 (0.25 = 5 mgs, 0.125= 2.5 mgs)	0.5
Clonazepam	Rivotril	24-100	1 mg
Zopiclone	Imovane	6.5	10 mg

Note: These dose equivalents are only approximate and may need to be adjusted to the patient's individual requirements.

Where there is an active metabolite, its half-life is shown in brackets.

Example 1: Changeover from Oxazepam (Serapax) to Diazepam

From a short-acting benzodiazepines to a long acting (Diazepam).
60 mgs of Oxazepam (Serapax) taken daily
Dose Equivalent of 60mg Oxazepam = 30 mgs Diazepam

Day One

	7am	12pm	3pm	6pm	10pm
Diaz:	2.5 mg				2.5 mg = **5 mg**
Oxa:	10 mg	10 mg	10 mg	10 mg	10 mg = **50 mg**

Day Two

	7am	12pm	3pm	6pm	10pm
Diaz:	2.5 mg				2.5 mg = **5 mg**
Oxa:	10 mg	10 mg	10 mg	10 mg	10 mg = **50 mg**

Day Three

	7am	12pm	5pm	10pm
Diaz:	2.5 mg	2.5 mg	2.5 mg	2.5 mg = **10 mg**
Oxa:	10 mg	10 mg	10 mg	10 mg = **40 mg**

Day Four

	7am	12pm	5pm	10pm
Diaz:	2.5 mg	2.5 mg	2.5 mg	2.5 mg = **10 mg**
Oxa:	10 mg	10 mg	10 mg	10 mg = **40 mg**

Day Five

	7am	12pm	5pm	10pm
Diaz:	5 mg	2.5 mg	2.5 mg	5 mg = **15 mg**
Oxa:	5 mg	10 mg	10 mg	5 mg = **30 mg**

Day Six

	7am	12pm	5pm	10pm
Diaz:	5 mg	2.5 mg	2.5 mg	5 mg = **15 mg**
Oxa:	5 mg	10 mg	10 mg	5 mg = **30 mg**

Day Seven

	7am	12pm	5pm	10pm
Diaz:	5 mg	5 mg	5 mg	5 mg = **20 mg**
Oxa:	5 mg	5 mg	5 mg	5 mg = **20 mg**

Day Eight

	7am	12pm	5pm	10pm
Diaz:	5 mg	5 mg	5 mg	5 mg = **20 mg**
Oxa:	5 mg	5 mg	5 mg	5 mg = **20 mg**

Day Nine

	7am	12pm	5pm	10pm
Diaz:	7.5 mg	5 mg	5 mg	7.5 mg = **25 mg**
Oxa:		5 mg	5 mg	= **10 mg**

Day Ten

	7am	12pm	5pm	10pm
Diaz:	7.5 mg	5 mg	5 mg	7.5 mg = **25 mg**
Oxa:		5 mg	5 mg	= **10 mg**

Day Eleven

	7am	12pm	5pm	10pm
Diaz:	7.5 mg	7.5 mg	7.5 mg	7.5 mg = **30 mg**
Oxa:				= **0 mg**

Example 2: Changeover from Imovane to Diazepam.

From a short acting minor tranquilliser to a long-acting Benzodiazepine (Diazepam)
Example: 22.5 mgs of Imovane (Zopiclone) daily.
Dose equivalent: 22.5 mgs Imovane = 22.5 mgs Diazepam

Day One

	7am	12pm	5pm	10pm
Diaz:	2.5 mg			5 mg = **7.5 mg**
Imov:	2.5 mg	2.5 mg	2.5 mg	7.5 mg = **15 mg**

Day Two

	7am	12pm	5pm	10pm
Diaz:	2.5 mg			5 mg = **7.5 mg**
Imov:	2.5 mg	2.5 mg	2.5 mg	7.5 mg = **15 mg**

Day Three

	7am	12pm	5pm	10pm
Diaz:	5 mg	2.5 mg	2.5 mg	5 mg = **7.5 mg**
Imov:				7.5 mg = **7.5 mg**

Day Four

	7am	12pm	5pm	10pm
Diaz:	5 mg	2.5 mg	2.5 mg	5 mg = **7.5 mg**
Imov:				7.5 mg = **7.5 mg**

Day Five

	7am	12pm	5pm	10pm
Diaz:	5 mg	5 mg	5 mg	7.5 mg = **22.5 mg**

Stabilisation and Restabilisation

Once the changeover is complete, you will need to stabilise for at least two weeks to adjust to the Diazepam before the reduction regimen is implemented.

You need:

- Time to re-energise without withdrawal symptoms.
- Time to adjust to the sedative effect of Diazepam.
- Time to normalise day to day living without withdrawal symptoms.
- Time to adjust to different sleeping patterns.

Diazepam accumulates during the day and holds you stable during sleep hours. It will also eliminate withdrawal symptoms upon waking.

Step 3: General Reduction Regime for Long Term Users (seven years and more)

HIGH DOSE 80 to 40 mg Diazepam Daily

- Reduce at 2.5 mg per week
- Hold for 4 –12 weeks to restabilise.

FROM 40 TO 20 mg Daily

- Reduce at 2.5 mg per fortnight.
- Hold for 4 to 12 weeks to restabilise.

FROM 20 TO 10 mg Daily

- Reduce at 2 mg every two to three weeks
- Hold for four to 12 weeks to restabilise.

FROM 10 TO 5 mg Daily

- Reduce at 1 mg per fortnight
- Hold for four to 12 weeks to restabilise.

FROM 5 mg TO nil Daily

- Reduce by 0.5 mg per fortnight until complete. In some cases, it may be necessary to reduce by 0.25 mg per fortnight.
- The lowest doses are the most difficult to reduce.

Step 3: Reduction - Shorter Term User (less than seven years)

The general rule is: it takes a month for every year on them to withdraw from them. For example, 30 years use requires a 30 month or approximately three-year detox. Seven years requires seven months detox. Adjustments need to be made for each individual, considering their other substance abuse/addiction, mental health issues, current life circumstances, and such. Reduction regimes will usually lie somewhere within this example:

HIGH DOSE From 80 to 40 mg Diazepam Daily
- Reduce at 5 mg every five to seven days
- Hold for two weeks to restabilise.

FROM 40 TO 20 mg Daily
- Reduce at 2.5 mg per week.
- Hold for two weeks to restabilise.

FROM 20 TO 10 mg Daily
- Reduce at 2 mg per week/fortnight
- Hold for 2-4 weeks to restabilise.

FROM 10 TO 5 mg Daily
- Reduce at 1 mg per week/fortnight
- Hold for two to four weeks to restabilise.

FROM 5 mg TO nil Daily
- Reduce by 0.5 mg per week/fortnight until complete.
- The lowest doses are the most difficult to reduce.

SUPPORT

Many people feel ashamed when they discover they have become addicted to benzodiazepines. It's important to remember that what you're experiencing is not your fault. Anyone can become addicted to benzodiazepines regardless of social status, race, religion, sex, or age. The best thing you can do is accept the problem, be courageous, love and nurture yourself, and take the necessary steps to make yourself well again. There are many things you can do to support and nurture yourself while withdrawing from benzodiazepines. There is help available and you don't have to do it alone.

Support Groups

Support groups are groups of people who have a similar problem and come together to support and encourage each other and share information about their problem. It's an opportunity to meet other people with similar issues and experiences. In the group you will be respected, encouraged, listened to, and understood.

Sharing Feelings

Even if you just sit and listen in a group you will learn a lot. Where else could you be in a relaxed atmosphere and say: "I've had a horrible week, I can't sleep, my muscles ache, and I have been feeling dreadful/horrible as if I'm going to die." Instead of getting strange looks, others will share the feelings and thoughts they are having in withdrawal. It can often be humorous, and humour is a wonderful way of relieving tension.

Who comes to Support Groups?

Men and women of all ages go to support groups. The stereotype of the middle-aged housewife is far from true. There is often a high number of men in their thirties and forties in the groups. Men can often feel more degraded than women and have often gone to great lengths to hide the truth of their symptoms from friends and family.

ADVICE TO HEALTH PROFESSIONALS

There has been concern for many years regarding Benzodiazepine addiction. The legislation (January 1999) has resulted in many long-time benzodiazepine users now trying to withdraw from these pills. There has been an increase in requests from health professionals for more information on benzodiazepine withdrawal.

It is important to note that withdrawal symptoms can and do occur with benzodiazepines following therapeutic doses given for a short period of time. Withdrawal symptoms include anxiety, tremors, confusion, depression, insomnia, perception disorders, fits, gastrointestinal and other somatic symptoms. These may be difficult to distinguish from the original disorder.

Withdrawal effects usually appear after stopping a benzodiazepine with a short half-life. Symptoms may continue for weeks or months. Addiction and withdrawal symptoms are not specific to certain types of benzodiazepines. The NZ Medicines Control Committee recommends that the use of benzodiazepines be limited in the following ways:

As Anxiolytics
Benzodiazepines are indicated for the short-term relief (two to four weeks only) of anxiety that is severe, disabling, or subjecting the individual to unacceptable distress,

occurring alone or in association with insomnia, or short-term psychosomatic, organic or psychotic distress. The use of benzodiazepines to treat short-term mild anxiety is inappropriate and unhelpful.

As Hypnotics
Benzodiazepines should only be used to treat insomnia when it is severe, disabling, or subjecting the individual to extreme distress.

Dosage
The lowest dose that can control the symptoms should be used. It should not be continued beyond four weeks. Long-term chronic use is not recommended. Treatment should always be tapered off gradually. Patients who have taken Benzodiazepines for a long time may require a longer period during which doses are reduced. When a Benzodiazepine is used as a hypnotic treatment, it should, if possible, be intermittent.

Precautions
Benzodiazepines should not be used alone to treat depression or anxiety associated with depression. Suicide may be precipitated in such patients. They should not be used for phobic or obsessional states. They should not be used to treat chronic psychosis. In the case of bereavement, psychological adjustment may be inhibited by benzodiazepines. Extreme caution should be used in prescribing benzodiazepines to patients with personality

disorders. Disinhibiting effects may manifest in various ways. Suicide can be precipitated in patients who are depressed, and aggressive behaviour towards self and others may also be precipitated.

JUDY'S STORY

Unlike your stereotypical drug addict, most benzo addicts are accidental addicts. They never set out to abuse or become addicted to drugs. They simply went to the doctor and complained of insomnia, anxiety or grief and were prescribed a minor tranquilizer. A shocking 70% of clients fronting up to Tranx Services fit into this category. Judy is typical of clients seen at Tranx; an attractive, 38-year-old, airline hostess who lives in the upmarket suburb with a husband and two kids.

Judy was prescribed Valium for anxiety, when she was just 18, her doctor told her it was not addictive. "Initially I thought yippee all my problems are solved." She had no idea she was in for a ten-year horrific battle with addiction. After six weeks she began to increase her dose to stop the shakes that had started in the morning.

Two years after starting Valium, Jude began her career as an airline hostess. Over the next eight years her daily dose would gradually increase from the initial 20 milligrams to a staggering 150 milligrams. Her pills never strayed far and she would take them every couple of hours. "The worst part was hiding my pills and the shakes that occurred as a result of withdrawal. My alcohol consumption increased dramatically and I felt more and more isolated. I contemplated suicide on a daily basis." Judy admits.

The problem eventually spiralled out of control when the pills no longer relieved her increasing anxiety. She stopped taking them and typically began to experience horrendous withdrawal symptoms; anxiety, panic, shakes, sweats, insomnia and depression. Ten years after starting Valium, Judy ended up in hospital after a neighbour found her collapsed on her floor. 'I knew I had to get off these things. I was petrified because of what I experienced when I tried to stop before. I went through a managed withdrawal in hospital. I had seizures and panic attacks and was expected to die. Luckily I didn't."

Jude's tale is not uncommon. Many people are completely unaware of just how addictive minor tranquilizers are. Doctors continue to prescribe tranquilizers for anxiety and insomnia, often bought on by real grief or depression. But you can't make grief disappear. Benzos just put it on ice for a while, but eventually you'll have to deal with it. Benzos are useful for short time periods while a person is in crisis. The therapeutic time frame is approximately three weeks.

MARCUS'S STORY

Benzos were considered primarily a middle class, female medication but the number of addicted males has increased; Marcus is a prime example. "My initial acquaintance with tranquilizers started when I was 31 and about to embark on a solo trip round the world. I guess I was just plain nervous and developed some unexplained chest pains. My doctor prescribed Serapax to help relax my muscles. I took them daily and the trip was a breeze.'

Returning to New Zealand, he resumed his teaching job in a large, expanding secondary school. It was an exciting job, but stressful at times. He suffered insomnia so asked his doctor for more Serepax and later more again. Marcus applied for a senior position. "Through the long gruelling interviews, I found popping 2 or 3 little yellow pills before interviews helped. I floated through the interviews eventually attaining the senior position. But by then I was taking 4 Serapax, 3-4 or more times daily."

He later developed arthritis and as the pain interfered with his sleep, the doctor added Halcion to the mix. "This started seriously affecting my relationships and life. I was moody, tense, and withdrawn. I wasn't sleeping. I was dissatisfied with life. The arthritis got worse and I got depressed. Another chat with my doctor and antidepressant (Prothieden) was added to the cocktail." This is a familiar pattern; a tranquilliser for day, a sleeping pill at night and an antidepressant when the patient inevitably starts feeling depressed.

Marcus, now in his late 40s can't go anywhere without Serapax in his pocket. It may seem apparent that Marcus is addicted, however he simply couldn't see it. "I was following the doctor's regime of tablets and thought it should be all right. It took a crisis to make me realize something was terribly wrong. I had to leave my job. I couldn't cope with the intense feelings I experienced, as well as the constant sweating, strange thoughts and muscle spasms in my neck and shoulders. I lost interest in friends and couldn't concentrate on bridge, my favourite pass time. My marriage suffered. I couldn't sit still at movies or meetings. I couldn't drive without panic attacks and sweats. My life became narrow and I'd completely changed."

By chance, Marcus found a Tranx Services pamphlet in a doctor's waiting room. He was disturbed to find that on 7 out of 10 counts he was an addict. After 18 years on these pills, that somehow came as a shock, Marcus laughs. "I won't bore you with the agonies of my withdrawal only to say that Tranx were absolute lifesavers. I'm now divorced, have moved from my old home and begun a completely new life. I've been off Benzos for 3 years now and hope never to take tranquilizers again. To anyone reading this who has been on Benzo's long term, I'd like to say, 'Yes you can get off them, but prepare for a struggle. It's hard but it's definitely worth it.'

USEFUL BOOKS & JOURNAL ARTICLES

There are many useful books and journal articles that have been written on benzodiazepine withdrawal.

Book List.

Coming off Tranquillisers, Sleeping pills and Antidepressants: A safe and effective withdrawal plan. Shirley Trickett, (1998), Caledonian International Book Manufacturers.

The Element Guide to Stress: Your Questions Answered. Rochelle Simmons, (1997). Element Books, Australia.

The Sky is Falling: Understanding and coping with Phobias, Panic and OCDs. Raeanne Dumont, (1997). W.W. Norton Publishers.

Panic Attacks: A Practical Guide to Recognising and Dealing with Feelings of Panic. Sue Bretan (1987), Random House.

The Eat Light Diet. Dr Peter D'Adamo, (1999), Random House.

The Anxiety and Phobia Workbook, 2nd Edition, Edmund, Bourne, Ph.D. (1999), New Harbinger Publications.

Thoughts and Feelings: Taking Control of your Moods and your Life. Matthew McKay, Ph.D., Martha Davis, Ph.D., Patrick Faming. (1997) Publishers Group West.

The Relaxation and Sleeping Reduction Workbook. 4th Edition, Martha Davis, Ph.D. Elizabeth Robbins, MSW, Matthew McKay, Ph.D. (1998) New Harbinger Publication.

The Depression Workbook: A guide for living with depression and manic depression. Mary Ellen Copeland, M.S. (1998) Peach Press.

Journal Articles.

Benzodiazepine, Dependence and Withdrawal: An update. Drug Newsletter, No 31, April 1985, Northern Regional Health Authority.

Benzodiazepines in General Practice: Time for a decision. J, Catalan, and D, H, Gath. British Medical Journal, Vol 290. 11 May 1985.

Benzodiazepine Withdrawal: An Unfinished Story. Heather Ashton, DM, FRCP, British Medical Journal, Vol. 288, 14 April 1984.

Benzodiazepine Withdrawal Outcome in 50 Patients. Heather Ashton, DM, FRCP. British Journal of Addiction, Vol 82, 1987, pp. 665-671.

Identification and Management of Benzodiazepine Dependence. P, Tyler and N, Sievewright. Postgraduate Medical Journal, Vol 60 (supplement 2), 1984, pp. 41-46.

www.ingramcontent.com/pod-product-compliance
Lightning Source LLC
Chambersburg PA
CBHW020331010526
44107CB00054B/2065